Editor-in-Chief and Founder:
  Lyndon H. LaRouche, Jr.
Editorial Board: *Lyndon H. LaRouche, Jr. , Helga
  Zepp-LaRouche, Robert Ingraham, Tony
  Papert, Gerald Rose, Dennis Small, Jeffrey
  Steinberg, William Wertz*
Co-Editors: *Robert Ingraham, Tony Papert*
Managing Editor: *Nancy Spannaus*
Technology: *Marsha Freeman*
Books: *Katherine Notley*
Ebooks: *Richard Burden*
Graphics: *Alan Yue*
Photos: *Stuart Lewis*
Circulation Manager: *Stanley Ezrol*

INTELLIGENCE DIRECTORS
Counterintelligence: *Jeffrey Steinberg, Michele
  Steinberg*
Economics: *John Hoefle, Marcia Merry Baker,
  Paul Gallagher*
History: *Anton Chaitkin*
Ibero-America: *Dennis Small*
Russia and Eastern Europe: *Rachel Douglas*
United States: *Debra Freeman*

INTERNATIONAL BUREAUS
Bogotá: *Miriam Redondo*
Berlin: *Rainer Apel*
Copenhagen: *Tom Gillesberg*
Houston: *Harley Schlanger*
Lima: *Sara Madueño*
Melbourne: *Robert Barwick*
Mexico City: *Gerardo Castilleja Chávez*
New Delhi: *Ramtanu Maitra*
Paris: *Christine Bierre*
Stockholm: *Ulf Sandmark*
United Nations, N.Y.C.: *Leni Rubinstein*
Washington, D.C.: *William Jones*
Wiesbaden: *Göran Haglund*

ON THE WEB
e-mail: eirns@larouchepub.com
www.larouchepub.com
www.executiveintelligencereview.com
www.larouchepub.com/eiw
Webmaster: *John Sigerson*
Assistant Webmaster: *George Hollis*
Editor, Arabic-language edition: *Hussein Askary*

EIR (ISSN 0273-6314) *is published weekly
(50 issues), by EIR News Service, Inc.,
P.O. Box 17390, Washington, D.C. 20041-0390.
(703) 777-9451 ext. 415*

European Headquarters: E.I.R. GmbH, Postfach
Bahnstrasse 9a, D-65205, Wiesbaden, Germany
Tel: 49-611-73650
Homepage: http://www.eirna.com
e-mail: eirna@eirna.com
Director: Georg Neudecker

Montreal, Canada: 514-461-1557

Denmark: EIR - Danmark, Sankt Knuds Vej 11,
basement left, DK-1903 Frederiksberg, Denmark.
Tel.: +45 35 43 60 40, Fax: +45 35 43 87 57. e-mail:
eirdk@hotmail.com.

Mexico City: EIR, Sor Juana Inés de la Cruz 242-2
Col. Agricultura C.P. 11360
Delegación M. Hidalgo, México D.F.
Tel. (5525) 5318-2301
eirmexico@gmail.com

Canada Post Publication Sales Agreement
#40683579

Postmaster: Send all address changes to *EIR*, P.O.
Box 17390, Washington, D.C. 20041-0390.

Signed articles in *EIR* represent the views of the
authors, and not necessarily those of the Editorial
Board.

I0407944

Build Up the People Destroyed by Bush and Obama

EDITORIAL

Edited excerpt of the final portion of Lyndon LaRouche and Helga Zepp-LaRouche's discussion with the La-Rouche PAC Policy Committee of Tuesday, Dec. 27.

Dave Christie: I have a question, which is, it looks like they're trying to sort of retool Obama for his after-Presidency. In other words, he's setting up his office at the World Wildlife Fund, and he did quite an insane interview where he claimed he could have beat Trump, and "the dream is still alive"; and such really narcissistic kind of rant. My thinking is that, first off, I think the American people have already said they reject Obama and they're not going to fall for it—but any idea of propping him up for some sort of afterlife or being active after the Presidency, would be in effect to intimidate the Democrats, because they never have broken with Obama, and therefore, they have fallen in line with everything that he represents in that sense.

So it would almost be to keep them in line. But on the other hand, here we have these war crimes that are being exposed, mass graves in Aleppo, and the ability to actually have Obama put in prison for these sorts of crimes,— well, we should do that I believe. But the question is, how much should that be an emphasis? In other words, as we try to move forward with the New Paradigm, how much effort do we actually want to expend, to have these Nazi forces in the United States brought down, like Obama? How much of an emphasis should there be on that?

Lyndon LaRouche: I don't think it'll work. The rejection of Obama, whose chief characteristic was his ability to kill citizens in the United States, regularly, that was his characteristic … When he is defeated, in a process of being defeated, he will disappear; or turn up in some prison some place. I wouldn't worry about it. I'd go at the positive things right away and build them up. That's what they need.

All the things that used to be skills, productive skills in the working classes—it's all been shattered, destroyed. We have to build up the people who were destroyed by what the Bush family and Obama did! That's the issue. Or we call it the New Bush League—what we're getting here, our option is the New Bush League. That means, at the end of Obama.

Helga Zepp-LaRouche: I thought it was funny that Newt Gingrich, who himself is a nasty fellow, used this image of an inflated doll; the air has gone out and it shrinks, and shrinks, and shrinks. That was my first image I had of Obama in 2008, in an editorial I wrote with the headline, "Obama, The Soufflé." [laughter] You know what happens to a soufflé when you treat it badly: it shrinks and collapses.

I agree. I think you should go with the new paradigm, and really go with the idea that we absolutely have to leave this era of misery of sixteen years of the Bush/Obama period behind us.

LaRouche: You have to do something about that Helga, also, just from the standpoint of your voice right now. You've got to get the people back to understanding what is available to them. We've got to break the ice on slavery, on various kinds and degrees of slavery inside the United States. And the ruin of our educational system, all these kinds of things. These things have to be rebuilt. Because it is those kinds of things which, when done properly, will lead the recovery of the United States population.

Zepp-LaRouche: Why don't we resume the Weekly [New Paradigm] Reports, and have a series of classes on Lyn's physical economy? All the discussion of Hamilton is fine, but Lyn is the author of physical economy, and we haven't really been discussing it in depth for quite some time.

Kesha Rogers: That's good, yes. That is the basis of what we discussed in our revamping of the Hamilton pamphlet,— to put the educational aspect around Lyn's conception of economics more up front, with the "Four Laws," and then the development around that.

I won't start that discussion until we're ready for it. But ...

Restore a Human Culture

Zepp-LaRouche: I don't just mean the Four Laws. I mean an in-depth economics class. Lyn has worked on this for 50 or 60 years, he has written numerous articles over this period, and there are a lot of conceptions in it which are not being talked about now, and we should absolutely revive them.

Benjamin Deniston: A few of us were looking back at what Lyn was doing around 2010, in fighting to upgrade people's understanding of the concept of infrastructure. And this led into the NAWAPA work, but at that time you first started developing the "platform" conception. I've been going back and rereading a number of your papers and some of the discussions from around that time, and I think there are a lot of very rich conceptions, and some very important conceptions, that we need to get across right now. Because there's all this talk about infrastructure, and about space, what the space policy should be, but a lot of it is not centered around any scientific conception.

And I think back to what you laid out at that time, for how to think about infrastructure as a sequence of successive stages or platforms. And you said that infrastructure is not an add-on, which is the way people normally think about it. Rather, it is the entire basis of your economy. It creates the actual synthetic environment in which the entire economy operates and which it depends upon. So when you're talking about creating new stages or levels of infrastructure platforms, it means creating anew an entire, higher-order, synthetic envi-

ronment that supports a completely new level of productivity of mankind.

So that's one arc of development which I think would be really critical to bring back in this exact context right now.

We were also talking about the point you made, Helga, going back as far as Lyn's conceptions around the Power of Labor, and that driving his economic discoveries. Lyn, you might have more to say about that. This goes to the question of how you came to understand the increases in relative potential population density. And these ideas that really shaped the development.

Zepp-LaRouche: Without the education of the labor force to a higher level of productivity, and naturally creativity, this cannot work. I mean by this, the tremendous deterioration of the cultural and moral level. I think you can contrast that with what Xi Jinping said about virtue and morality being the key to having the right attitude on the education question. And Putin spoke earlier about how the West has completely deteriorated culturally by throwing out all human values and replacing them with perversions. If you don't correct that, I don't think you can get the kind of productive labor force that is required—because if people are still pornographic in their thinking and full of admiration for violence, how can they be creative? They cannot.

And that is something which is completely lacking in the discussion. At least I haven't heard anybody other than us talking about it.

How To Inspire Creativity

LaRouche: Look at the Franklin Roosevelt administration's pioneering of a new way to greater advantages for the people of the United States and elsewhere. Take the way that worked. You have to realize how much, afterwards, was put into destroying the skills, and the minds of the skilled labor force generally, at the end World War II. Everything went rotten. The worst thing we had was not World War II, but the rottenness of the U.S. labor force critics who crushed the financial functions of the labor force. And I know that *cold*, detail by detail, with bitter memory.

Zepp-LaRouche: Just remember, the oligarchy can't exist if they have an intelligent population, so the moment Roosevelt was dead, the Truman administration really moved in to destroy the axioms which had made Roosevelt possible; and one of their devices was the Congress for Cultural Freedom, which had the deliberate aim of uprooting people from Classical music—Theodor Adorno, the Frankfurt School, and the Congress for Cultural Freedom, they all tried to completely destroy,— on the one side to destroy the Classical tradition, but then also destroy what little was left of the Classical tradition to replace it with ugliness. Furtwängler was replaced with Herbert von Karajan, and the right interpretation was thrown out of the window; modern music was mixed with Classical music so that people would just not build up their concentration span. All of these things went into really downgrading the population over a long period of time.

LaRouche: Yes!

Zepp-LaRouche: And that has to be reversed.

Science-Driver Is the Starting Point

Deniston: One reference point we've often looked to for the general idea of educating and training the labor force, was Roosevelt's Civilian Conservation Corps (CCC) program. I wonder if we could look at that, and how it would need to be expanded, possibly including some of these aspects of Classical education and musical training. What Lyn just said is critical: that we're obviously dealing with a deeper and longer degeneration than Franklin Roosevelt dealt with. You must also look at the drug crisis. I think we need to put more thought into all of this: how we actually uplift this population as a whole, and get it trained to the point where it can be productive and creative.

And if we're seriously talking about pursuing this whole program, and we don't have that defined, then people are not going to believe us unless we have a real idea and a road map of what it's going to take to transform the population. It might take a generation or more to really do …

Zepp-LaRouche: And if you look at all of the university teaching: Science has been replaced with algorithms; economic theory is just neoliberal monetarism; medicine is health economics—all of these subjects have been completely distorted. History is the history of imperial order interpretation … You can look at practically every field, and you find that there has been tremendous distortion.

LaRouche: But most of the people of the United States have been brainwashed. And I do mean, literally, brainwashed. And that's the thing you've got to correct. You've got to bring people *who are actually ignorant*, not just ignorant of particular things, but ignorant in their behavior towards society in general. And if we want to win this, win a recovery of the U.S. economy, you've got to do that.

Zepp-LaRouche: But it's the same thing in Germany, except that here the ignorance is paired with arrogance.

LaRouche: We've got the arrogance all over the place; it's not here, it's all over the place! Every idiot is his own genius! [laughter]

Deniston: From the standpoint of my understanding of Lyn's principles of economics, it seems that the starting point should be the science-driver program, the space program and fusion …

LaRouche: Yes. Yes!

Deniston: And the challenge is then linking that all throughout the economy as a whole, because that creates the framework in which you need to uplift the middle class, and the lower class, the downtrodden, to participate in an economy that's organized as a whole from that standpoint.

LaRouche: I think we have the latent option—in the United States for example—I think we have a latent option for this. I think we can probably get that back again, and can push away the kind of thing that destroyed the financial system, the U.S. financial system, when President Franklin Roosevelt was crushed. It was that simple. And this is what you've got to have, the leadership which goes—like Franklin Roosevelt's campaigns—to the issue of what is necessary to instruct people to recognize what will make them better in terms of their behavior in society.

Rogers: Right. I think that's very good, because it gives a real direction for the thinking process of our organization as a whole, and what we're actually out to create.

LaRouche: Yes. Being an old man, I know a lot of

the things which are not secrets, but they were poisonous nonetheless!

Zepp-LaRouche: Yes, and no matter what the Trump team may do, they may even go after drugs, and they may do this and that, but the positive thing, I cannot see where it can come from, unless we inject it.

LaRouche: Yes. You have to educate people by using the kinds of tools of education which make them creative. That used to happen in the United States; that used to happen. And then it went down, when Franklin Roosevelt dropped out. But now we've seen everything, all the dirty business in the United States is still there, and it has to be removed. In other words, all these things from the people who were opposed to Franklin Roosevelt—that has to be removed and a vision of what Franklin Roosevelt accomplished, in a decade, particularly—that's what has to be created, and what things must be based on.

Zepp-LaRouche: Okay, good! So, let's work on these things.

EIR Contents

www.larouchepub.com Volume 43, Number 53, December 30, 2016

Cover This Week

An Experiment on a Bird in the Air Pump *(1768) Joseph Wright of Derby*

BUILD UP THE PEOPLE DESTROYED BY BUSH AND OBAMA

A Global Revolution Is Outflanking Obama and the British Empire

The following is an edited version of remarks given by Michael Billington on the Dec. 23, 2016 LaRouche PAC Weekly Webcast.

I'm certainly glad to be here. It is an incredible moment in history; it reminds me of the opening of Dickens' *A Tale of Two Cities,* where he says, "It was the best of times, it was the worst of times . . ." He meant it, and it's true; we are in a revolutionary period, there's no question about that. This is sweeping the globe. It's already largely taken over Asia, and the Brexit, the Italian vote, and the Trump vote, indicate that people have finally reached the limit to the power of tyranny over their economy, over perpetual warfare. But a revolution doesn't necessarily have a positive outcome, and that's actually what Dickens was talking about. The French Revolution came soon after the historic and wonderful American Revolution, which was based on a new conception of man, based upon science and technology, and a new financial system under Hamilton's ideas, to defeat the power of the British Empire, which lay in their global financial empire.

The French Revolution was taken over actually by the British, and turned into chaos. It's what Schiller said: "A great moment has found a little people." So, instead of a great republic, you ended with the guillotine; you ended up with Robespierre saying the revolution has no need for science, and ultimately this led to the emergence of the first fascist—Napoleon. So, we cannot be complacent. We have a tremendous victory in the defeat of Obama and his clone, Hillary, and their British operation. But we certainly cannot sit back and cross our fingers and hope that Trump is going to do the

LaRouche PAC TV

Michael Billington

right thing. It's going to be up to us.

We should reflect on how the American Revolution succeeded. It succeeded because it was focussed on a tremendous sense of history and philosophical thought. The Founding Fathers put together the *Federalist Papers,* as well as the writings of Alexander Hamilton, which we've recently published. If you read these—which are not easy—this was the basis on which the so-called common men and women studied and came to the conclusion that, in fact, this small group of leaders were leading them in the right direction, and were creating a future. It was based on poetry.

In fact, Schiller was known as the Poet of Freedom and was treasured for 100 years after the American Revolution, as the poet of the American Revolution, despite being German and writing in German. But this was known to the American people. The music of the great *Messiah* by Handel, which was composed in 1741, it was known. Our Schiller Institute just performed a phenomenal version of this great work—the *Messiah*—at the Co-Cathedral of St. Joseph in Brooklyn Dec. 17, 2016, in an extremely moving ceremony. These are the kinds of ceremonies that took place at the time of the American Revolution, that lifted people to a higher sense of their humanity, of the dignity of man, and of creating a future.

So, which of these two paths are we going to be taking today? Well, it's obvious which way Obama was going. We've made that very clear. His intention was war; not only the perpetual wars in the Middle East, but leading to a war with Russia and a war with China. These are not completely resolved, but we are now a long way away from that horror which was facing us, had we not defeated that in this election.

But the result of these sixteen years of Bush and Obama can be seen in what's happened to our own country—not just the Hell that's been taken to the Middle East and other parts of the world. We now have a decline in life expectancy for the first time in our nation's history. We have a drug epidemic in which 1 out of 15 Americans is addicted to heroin or its substitutes: 1 out of 15 Americans! This is not a problem—this is a disaster, a collapse of civilization which is not only tolerated but supported openly by our President, who promotes legalizing drugs, and who is doing everything in his power to stop the emergence of a war on drugs in the Philippines, which I'll come back to.

Vladimir Putin's Leadership

On the other hand, we see that Russia, under Putin's direction, has intervened to stop this series of regime-change operations. What's happened in the tremendous victory in Aleppo against terrorism, is that Putin has demonstrated that if you work hand-in-hand with sovereign nations, and with their leaders, you can defeat terrorism. And he basically exposed the fact that Obama—like Bush—was on the side of the terrorists. Under the guise of fighting terrorism, Obama was openly working with the Saudis and the British, who

were arming and creating these terrorist movements to overthrow regimes who refused to follow their dictates—the so-called "regime-change" movement. That's probably been crushed. This is not completely solved, but what's happened in Aleppo not only stops the disintegration of Syria, but it should—if properly pursued—mean the end of the regime-change criminality of both Bush and Obama once and for all.

Today happened to be the day that Putin gave his annual end-of-year press conference. I think just reading one section of part of that, and paraphrasing a few others is important. It's important for people to watch Putin. It's done with an English voice-over. It's useful to watch to see why it is that the oligarchy is so terrified of this man.

I'm just going to read you—actually it was a question that came from a man named Yevgeny Primakov, and it turns out that he is, indeed, the grandson of the great Yevgeny Primakov, who died recently, and who was the original architect of the idea of China, Russia, and India collaborating to form a new core of nations that could appeal to America to join them. This is, of course, what has to happen, as a basis for reversing the imperially dictated decline of the human race. This initial multination formation led to the BRICS, and to the New Silk Road.

So, his grandson asked a question which said, "Mr. Putin, Barack Obama, who is still your official colleague, said that 37% of the Republicans sympathize with you, and that hearing this, Ronald Reagan would have rolled over in his grave.... Our western colleagues often tell us that you have the power to manipulate the world, to designate Presidents and to interfere in elections here and there. How does it feel to be the most powerful person on Earth? Thank you."

With that humorous, but very insightful question, Putin said the following:

> The current U.S. Administration and leaders of the Democratic Party are trying to blame all their failures on outside factors....
>
> We know that not only did the Democratic Party lose the presidential election, but also the Senate, where the Republicans have the majority, and Congress, where the Republicans are also in control. Did we, or I also do that?...
>
> It seems to me there is a gap between the elitist vision of what is good and bad and that of what in earlier times we would have called the

broad popular masses.... A substantial part of the American people share similar views with us on the world's organization, what we ought to be doing, and the common threats and challenges we are facing. It is good that there are people who sympathize with our views on traditional values, because this forms a good foundation on which to build relations between two such powerful countries as Russia and the United States, build them on the basis of our peoples' mutual sympathy.

... I'm not so sure who might be turning in their grave right now. It seems to me that Reagan would be happy to see his party's people winning everywhere, and would welcome the victory of the newly elected President so adept at catching the public mood, and who took precisely this direction and pressed onwards to the very end, even when no one except us believed he could win.

The outstanding Democrats in American history would probably be turning in their graves though. Roosevelt certainly would be, because he was an exceptional statesman in American and world history, who knew how to unite the nation even during the Great Depression's bleakest years, in the late 1930s, and during World War II. Today's administration, however, is very clearly dividing the nation. The call for the electors not to vote for either candidate—in this case, not to vote for the President-elect, was quite simply a step towards dividing the nation. Two electors did decide not to vote for Trump, and four not to vote for Clinton, and here too they lost. They are losing on all fronts and looking for scapegoats on whom to lay the blame. I think that this is an affront to their own dignity. It is important to know how to lose gracefully.

Helga Zepp-LaRouche commented when I read this to her, that this is a call not only to the Democrats in America, but to the oligarchs throughout the world who are acting as if this revolutionary change is not taking

EIRNS/Stefan Tolksdorf

Helga Zepp-LaRouche in China Sept. 29, 2015, to introduce the Chinese translation of EIR*'s report,* The New Silk Road Becomes the World Land-Bridge.

place, as if they still have the power to dictate policies, and who are hysterical about what is happening in America.

Putin concludes this way. He says:

> But my real hope is for us to build businesslike and constructive relations with the new President and with the future Democratic Party leaders as well, because this is in the interests of both countries and peoples.

So, this is leadership—what we so sorely miss here in the United States. There's much more; more will be made available in the *EIR.*

Breathtaking Developments in Asia

Now let me turn to Asia. Asia today should—in fact China in particular, but not just China—should be seen as the model which America must follow if we are to pull ourselves out of the morass that we're in today. We've discussed this in this program and in our publications many times: the entire Silk Road development—the development of corridors. I want to put some maps up, and just very quickly review some of the incredible development projects that are going on, virtually every single day.

On this map you can see the original corridor, which

Southern Asia and Its Neighbors

was the Trans-Siberian Railroad [**Fig. 1**, Corridors E], developed with consultation and advice from Henry Carey, who worked with the Russians to replicate what had been done in the United States with our Transcontinental Railroad, not just to go from one end to the other, but to develop the entire region in between.

Now, you see the lower one that goes through China, through Xinjiang Province, into Kazakhstan [Fig. 1, Corridor F]. This is the New Silk Road, which was developed following the 1990s, with the fall of the Soviet Union. Helga Zepp-LaRouche helped organize, in Beijing, a conference in 1996 on what the Chinese call the "New Eurasian Land-Bridge." Helga called it the "New Silk Road" even then.

This led to the building of this Asian rail network which is now functioning. It has several branches, both in China, and, on the far side, in Europe, as well as branches down into Central Asia. It's being upgraded. It's not properly connected, it doesn't all have the same gauge, and most of it is not high-speed. So this is a work-in-process.

Now look at what's happened just in the last few years. This is what's called the Pakistan Corridor. This is a connection by rail, from China, down through Pakistan, into Baluchistan (the southern part of Pakistan), and to the Gwadar Port, which is

being transformed into a major hub for oil from the Middle East, for trade with India—hopefully, the India/Pakistan relationship can be resolved. Then right around here in southern Iran, is the development of the Chabahar Port, from which there are rail connections up through Iran to Teheran, and then into Azerbaijan, and into Russia: [here is] another north/south route. As a result, you have several north/south routes.

Over here, you see a line that goes from Kunming in southern China, through Thailand, Myanmar, and into India. This is the old Burma Road that was built during the Second World War. Mr. Lyndon LaRouche had a hand in building the Burma Road (or worked along that Road). That's now being reconstructed. It will eventually be a rail connection. And a pipeline extends from China all the way down to the coast of Myanmar, where they are now taking in shipments of Middle East oil and piping it up into China.

Over here, this corridor. You already have rail connections from Kunming down to the Laos border, and now the Chinese are building a high-speed rail through Laos, down to the Thai border. Just in the last few months, they've concluded their plans to build a high-speed rail line from the Laos border down to Bangkok. At this point, there's only an old railroad from Bangkok down to Kuala Lumpur in Malaysia. But that will eventually be done; and in the meantime, probably the Chi-

Creative Commons

Premier of the People's Republic of China Zhou Enlai (left) with Egyptian Head of State Gamal Abdel Nasser (center) and other delegates at the April 18-24, 1955 Asian-African Conference in Bandung, Indonesia.

FIGURE 1

The World Land-Bridge Network—Key Links and Corridors

*Committed, underway or completed.

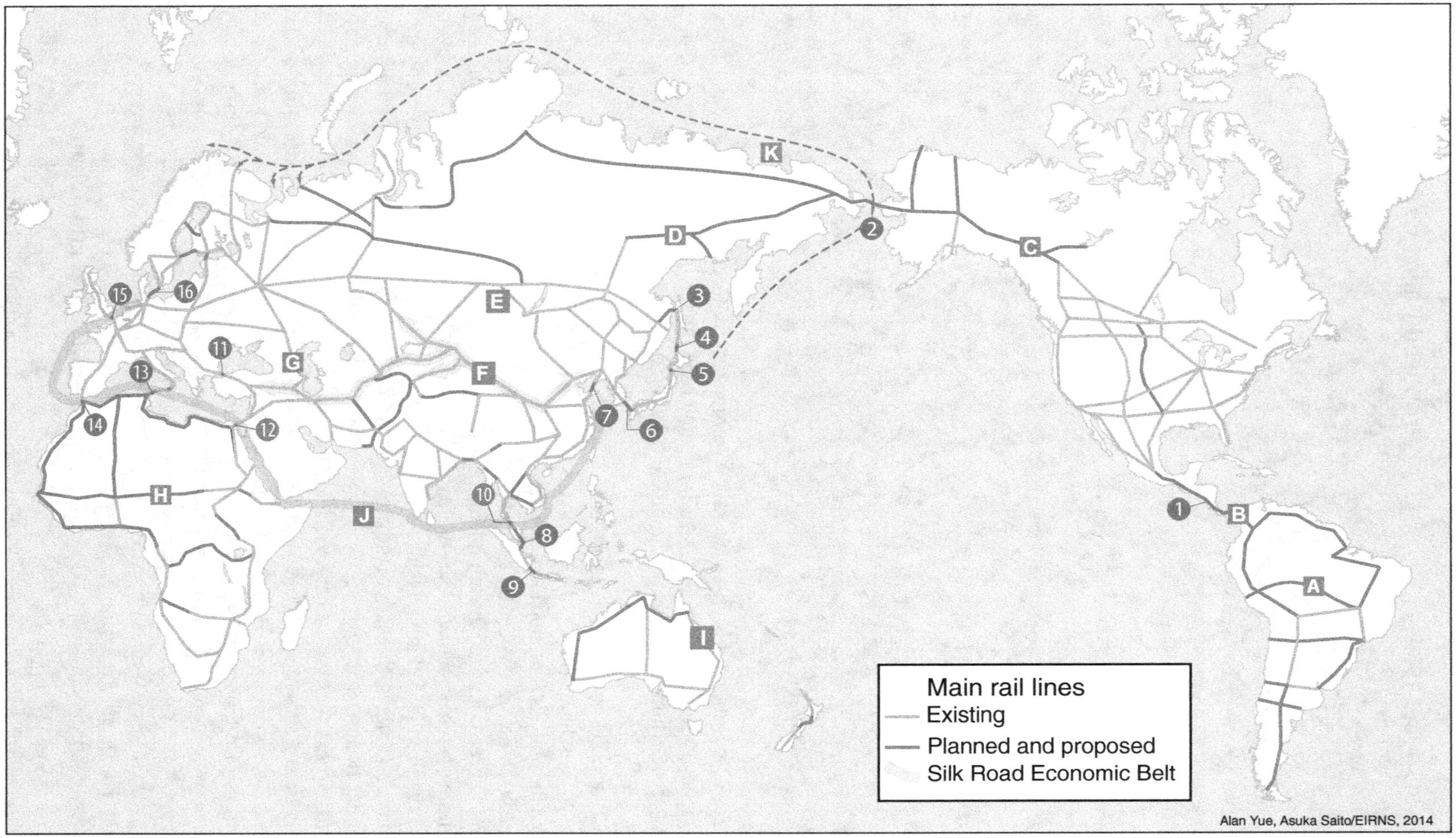
K
D
C
E
F
G
H
J
I
B
A
1
2
3
4
5
6
7
8
9
10
11
12
13
14
15
16
Main rail lines
Existing
Planned and proposed
Silk Road Economic Belt
Alan Yue, Asuka Saito/EIRNS, 2014

LINKS

1. *Great Inter-Oceanic Canal, Nicaragua
2. Bering Strait Tunnel
3. Sakhalin Island-Mainland (Russia) Connection
4. Sakhalin-Hokkaido Tunnel
5. *Seikan Tunnel
6. Japan-Korea Undersea Tunnel
7. *Bohai Tunnel
8. Strait of Malacca Bridge
9. Sunda Strait Bridge
10. Isthmus of Kra Canal
11. *Bosporus Strait Rail Tunnel
12. *Suez Canal Expansion
13. Italy-Tunisia Link
14. Strait of Gibraltar Tunnel
15. *English Channel Tunnel
16. *Scandinavian-Continental Links

CORRIDORS

- A *Peru-Brazil Transcontinental Railway
- B Darien Gap Inter-American Railway
- C Alaska-Canada-Lower 48 Rail Line
- D The Bering Strait Connector
- E Trans-Siberian Corridors
- F *Silk Road Economic Belt
- G *International North-South Transport Corridor
- H *Cross Africa Rail Lines
- I Australia Ring Railway
- J *Maritime Silk Road
- K *Northern Sea Route

Note: Geographical locations and corridors are shown schematically, with more than one railway combined as a single line in cases where major routes are parallel and in proximity. Maps within chapters of this report show greater detail.

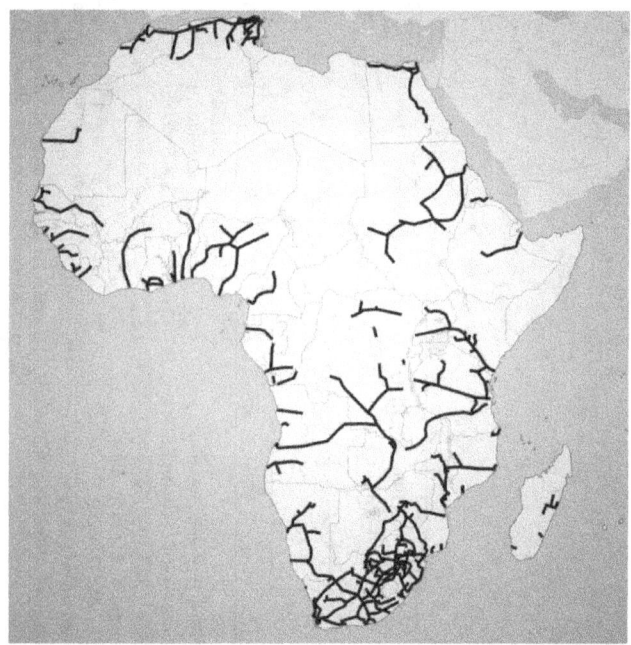

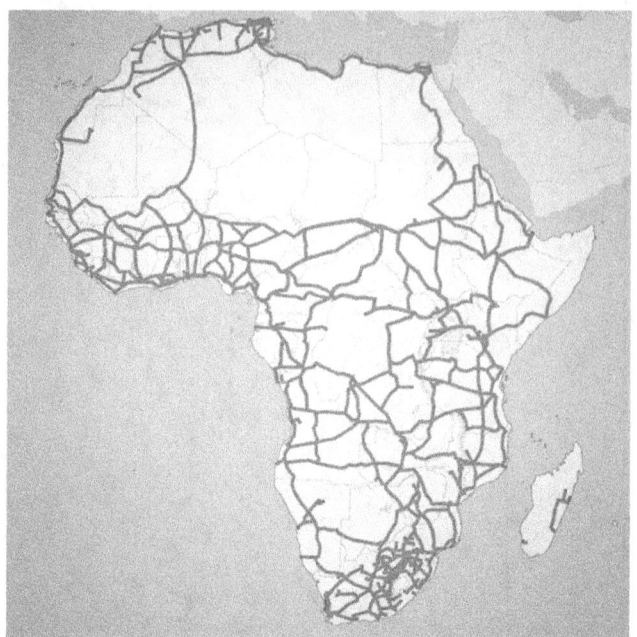

EIRNS/Fusion Energy Foundation, 1980

Existing railroads in Africa in 1980 (left) compared to a continent-wide proposal made by the Fusion Energy Foundation in 1980.

nese, maybe the Japanese, will build a high-speed rail from Kuala Lumpur to Singapore. So, eventually, you'll have this all the way from Kunming down to Singapore.

In Indonesia, the Chinese are building a railroad from the capital of Jakarta to Bandung. Many of you have heard of Bandung from the famous Bandung Conference in 1955, which was the first meeting of Asian and African leaders who had formerly been colonized, meeting without their colonial masters—the so-called Asia-Africa Conference that was organized by Sukarno, Nehru, and Zhou Enlai (from China), and others. So that's in the process, along with other developments there.

As for Africa, go to the next slide with the two Africa maps. This [**Fig. 2**] is from *EIR*'s report *The New Silk Road Becomes the World Land-Bridge*. This shows the existing rail structures as of a few years ago. You see that basically there's no way to get from one capital to another. You can only get the raw materials from the mine out to the port, where they were shipped off to Europe and America. That's all the colonial powers cared about in developing Africa.

What you see here, is a general map of the kind of commitment that the Chinese have made to connect every capital of Africa with high-speed rail, with sev-

eral cross-continental railroads. The Chinese need raw materials, just like the Europeans did, but they're paying for it; they're building nations. They're building nations that have industry, agriculture, water, power, and education, using a model which we used to call the American System, but which we've deserted in our country.

The same in South America. You can go to the next map [**Fig. 3**] here. This is also from our report. The Chinese are talking about building two trans-oceanic railroads: one that goes from Peru directly into Brazil and to the coast; one that goes south of that through Bolivia. The Bolivians, of course, want that railroad to go through Bolivia.

So, again, we see a transforming of the world in a way which, of course, the United States long ago ceased to do, becoming more of a British-style colonial power which looted the raw materials, imposing huge amounts of debt, and then using that debt as a weapon to keep the countries in a state of backwardness.

The Philippines and Japan

Now, I'm going to look at two other aspects of Asia—the Philippines and Japan—where huge transformations are taking place. Most of you have seen—

FIGURE 3
South America: Great Rail and Agricultural Projects

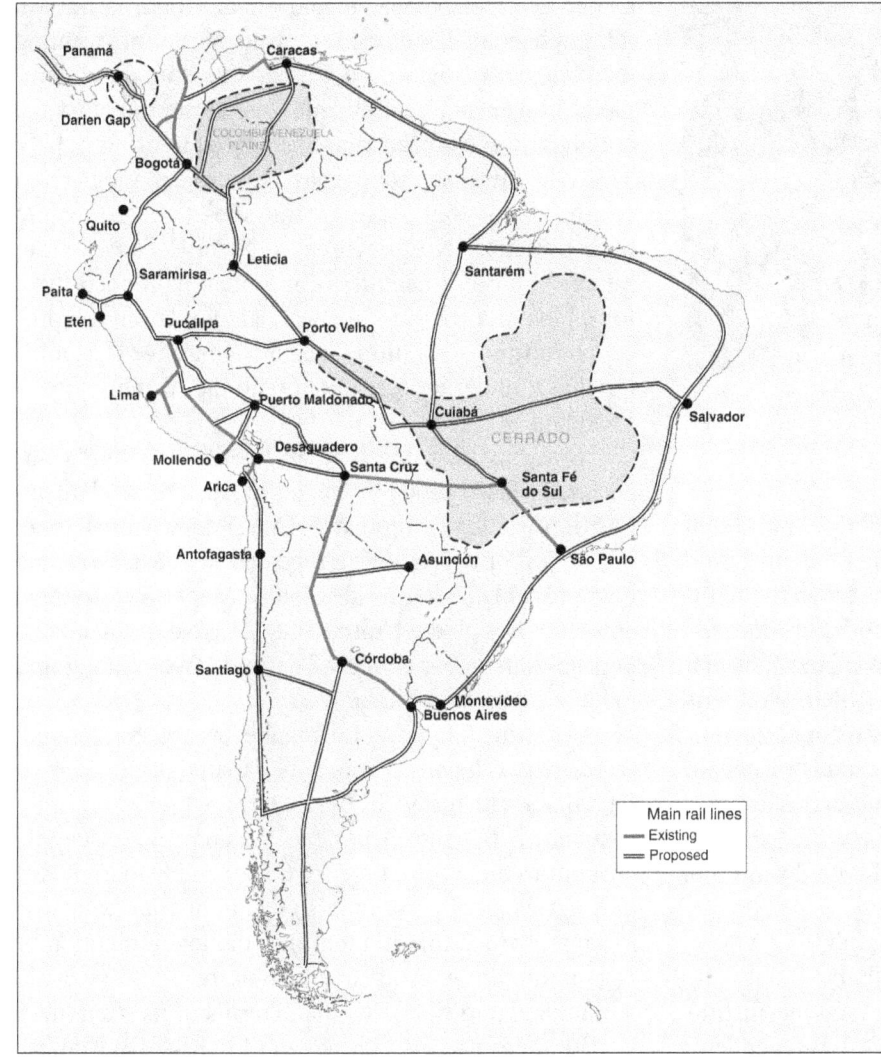

frastructure projects. They had built rail and road infrastructure.

There's Imelda Marcos, whom most of you know only because she supposedly was wildly extravagant and had millions of pairs of shoes. Well, the reason she had the shoes was because she built a shoe industry in the Philippines. She brought in Italian shoemakers, she shipped in cattle from Australia, for the leather, and she created a shoe industry.

Those who produced the shoes in the Philippines were so grateful that they gave her the first pair of any new shoe they developed. That's the reality, contrary to the "fake news" that we received back in the 1980s, when the neocons, under George Schultz and others, decided to overthrow Marcos, so as to make a horrible example of him: that they would not allow Third World countries to have nuclear power, or to be self-sufficient.

The result is, that what was once the greatest rising power in Southeast Asia, has become the basket case of that region. And this is what Duterte is acknowledging. He's saying, "We've been destroyed by the so-called big brother, who looks down at the 'little brown brothers' in the Philippines." And he said, in effect, "We're not going to tolerate it any more. We're going to crush the drugs that have been brought into our country and are destroying our children. And we're going to reject the U.S. domination of our economy, where all they want is our raw materials, and to use our bright young people who graduate from college, who have no jobs as engineers, scientists or teachers, or nurses or doctors—but who can only work all night long in call-centers, answering calls from the master back in the United States who has a problem with his computer or his banking code." This is how the country was destroyed.

So, he's turned to China and to Russia. His Defense Minister, Delfin Lorenzana, has gone to Russia, and

either in our material or just in the daily news—about Rodrigo Duterte, the new Philippine President who took office in June of this year, and who has totally transformed the Philippines, with massive, massive support from the population, estimated at more than 80%.

Why? It's because he took on the reality that the country had been destroyed. The history of the Philippines, in brief, was that in the 1970s and 1980s, they were viewed by the rest of Asia—including Korea, by the way—as the model for development, under their President Ferdinand Marcos. They had built the first nuclear power plant. They had made the country self-sufficient in rice, by direct support for infrastructure for agriculture. They had built eleven major industrial in-

Imelda Marcos created a shoe industry in Philippines. She is shown here with the first pair of every shoe model produced in the Philippines, which was presented to her as a gift.

Duterte is going to China. They're going to build that country. They're going to end this drug epidemic. And for that, he's being told he's going to be taken to the International Criminal Court for extra-judicial murders, for human rights violations—because of the fact that drug dealers who fight back are being killed. Well, this is rather hypocritical, I would say, if you count the tens of thousands, indeed hundreds of thousands of people that Obama has killed through extrajudicial murder—no court, no due process, no proof. Just, the king decides: "This is my list of people to kill with drones this week."

Obama and John Brennan, Director of the CIA do it. This is rather hypocritical. What's really behind it? The British don't want to stop drugs. The banking institutions in London and New York are drug-dependent, meaning they're drug-money dependent, in addition to the fact that many of the bankers are high on cocaine and heroin. They're drug dependent in the sense that the biggest business in the world, illegal narcotics, is propping up these bankrupt Western banks who do nothing but speculate. This is the reality of these big banks.

And of course, the main thing is that they don't want to see this war on drugs brought home. One out of every fifteen Americans is addicted to heroin. This is mind-boggling! And they know that the American people—if they're given a sense of who is responsible, like we did with our War on Drugs policy under LaRouche's direction back in the '80s and '90s—that this could capture the minds of the American people.

Lastly, let me mention Japan. The British-American strategy for containing China and Russia on the Asian side, has always been through South Korea, Japan, the Philippines, and Australia. And Singapore is in there someplace. Many of you know that Korea is now in total upheaval. The President, who started off wanting to work with Russia and China, was somehow completely taken over by Obama, and turned against the collaboration with Eurasia. She agreed to bring in U.S. THAAD missiles, supposedly to protect them from North Korea—but these are missiles that go up into high altitudes. North Korea is 30 miles away from Seoul. You don't need this for Korea! You need them for China and Russia—for war. They were in the process of turning the Philippines into a massive U.S. military base, under an agreement with the former puppet-President.

Now, however, the Korean President is being impeached. She'll probably be out in April or so. The opposition wants to stop that THAAD deployment. And, in the Philippines, Duterte repeated just last week that he's probably going to absolutely cancel the strategic agreements with the United States. "We don't need foreign soldiers in our country," he said. "We're not going to have a war with China."

As to Japan, Lyndon LaRouche has always said that there are two Japans. There's the Japan that came out of feudalism with the Meiji Restoration, which was highly influenced by the American System. Key people brought in the work of Henry Carey and Friedrich List in America, giving rise to this great industrial explosion in Japan, which turned them into the leading nation of Asia at that time, even superseding the 5,000-year-old culture and tradition in China in terms of its strength.

But there was also the Japan of the British Empire; the British came at the same time, and basically said, "Look, Japan, you're an island nation like we are. You need to get raw materials; you don't have them in your own country. The only way you're going to get them is by having a mighty military, and colonizing—taking over countries and taking their raw materials like we have—the great British Empire." Without going through all the details, as you know, this eventually won out, in the sense that Japan adopted a militarist policy and unleashed the horror of the Second World War, which started in Asia long before Pearl Harbor. It started with the invasion of China and the looting of China, leading to the destruction of China and other countries, and ultimately to the destruction of Japan itself.

President Shinzo Abe represents both of these

things. He has had his problems with China; he has wanted to remilitarize to get out from under the Constitution in Japan, which forbade Japan to fight war, a Constitution worked out after World War II with General Douglas MacArthur's collaboration. But, he also recognizes that he's gotten nothing from the collapsing Western financial system, and he sees the future of Japan in the real development of Russia and China, and of Asia generally—not by taking it over this time, but by collaboration through the New Paradigm, through the New Silk Road, and through collaboration especially with Russia. His grandfather, who was a Prime Minister, and his father, who was a politician, were committed to developing good relations with Russia, and Prime Minister Shinzo Abe is now on that course.

K. Rodriguez of the Philippine Presidential Department.

Philippine President Rodrigo Duterte (left) being greeted by China President Xi Jinping prior to their bilateral meetings in Beijing, Oct. 20, 2016.

The Russian-Japanese Rapprochement

So, what's happened this year? It's an extraordinary transformation taking place. It began with Abe's visit to Putin in Sochi in May, when Abe laid out an eight-point program for the development of the Russian Far East using Japanese technology, resources, and financing. Also, in May, there was a meeting of the G-7 in Japan. Russia wasn't there, because Obama had thrown Russia out of the G-8; it became the G-7 again. So, he didn't meet Putin there. But at that event, Abe basically said to the other G-7 leaders—including Obama—that the G-7 nations are on the brink of a horrible financial breakdown crisis, a crisis worse than that of 2008.

This analysis was absolutely rejected. Obama said, "No, we're in a recovery; it might be too slow, but it's going well." What Obama didn't say publicly is that, because there is a lot of money being printed to keep the speculation going in the banks, and there are lots of drugs flowing everywhere, that things are going fine for the bankers.

So, Abe was crushed on that; the final communiqué didn't mention what Abe had said, but everybody knew. Then, in September, he went to Vladivostok for a conference organized by Putin on the development of Russia's Far East, and they went further ahead with these development projects. And then finally, this month,

Putin came to Japan. He went to Yamaguchi, Abe's hometown. He then went to Tokyo. He visited the karate teacher that had awarded Putin one of the great black belts. But nevertheless, they knew they would not be able to overcome the still-festering problem of the territorial issue of the so-called Northern Territories, or the Kuril Islands.

At the very end of the Second World War, when the Russians had come in to help with the war in Japan, they had taken the Kurils, which had gone back and forth throughout history. These are basically four islands north of Japan. Both sides claim sovereignty; the Japanese want them back. What Abe and Putin agreed to was that they would go with a policy that had first been put forward in 1956 to divide the islands two and two. That 1956 agreement had been stopped by the United States, when the Dulles brothers came in and said, "Don't you dare; you must demand all of these islands back from the Russians, or else we won't turn Okinawa back to you."

So, the Japanese backed away from that deal, and after that, the Russians said, "OK, that's it. You're not going to get any of them back." So, now Putin has said, "OK, we can start joint development of these four islands. Joint development. And over time, we can go back to the 1956 agreement and come to a settlement, meaning that we'll be able to finally have a peace settlement to World War II," probably by 2018.

But in the meantime, Russia and Japan have already

A Terminal High Altitude Area Defense (THAAD) interceptor in a Nov. 1, 2015 test.

true now. We're at a moment which is going to go one way or the other. It's going to depend on you and me, on making sure that we take this fight now at a crucial moment—what Schiller called a great moment—and make sure that we define a future that uplifts people to a level of the dignity of their true humanity through activating the creative powers that they have by the right of being human beings created in the image of God.

This is our task, and this is where we stand today, and it's a great time to be celebrating Christmas, but you should be thinking about George Washington leading the fight across the Delaware River on Christmas Eve. That's the way we have to approach the fight that we have on our hands today. A good fight, one that gives us reason to be happy, but which is deadly serious.

Thank you.

initiated huge development projects. They made agreements for $2.5 billion of infrastructure projects throughout the Russian Far East—ports, rail, agriculture, nuclear, pharmaceuticals, education, cultural exchanges, and a $1 billion joint fund which can be leveraged into more, within this new framework for peace. So, just as Putin has largely unified the entire Middle East (he's even now talking to Bibi Netanyahu and the Saudis, because he's in charge—Obama and the British game is largely defeated) so, too in Asia, the China Silk Road process, the new financial institutions, and the development projects are bringing all of these nations together. There are still a few problems, but it's a new world. It's a new world which the United States can and must join. It's the only option.

A word of caution: While Obama's "Pivot to Asia" is dead, the Trans-Pacific Partnership (TPP) is dead, and the regime-change policies are largely dead, it would be a deadly mistake to just sit back and say, "Yahoo! Trump's going to do it for us!" That is not the case. This is going to be done by us. We created the environment in America and around the world which made it possible for these revolutionary changes to take place.

It's the power of ideas that moves history; it's Lyndon LaRouche and Helga Zepp-LaRouche and this institution that fought for these ideas before they became popular. In other words, we fought to bring these ideas into circulation, which made possible the emergence of people who recognized the truth of those ideas and have begun to take them up. This is doubly

The Multiple Dimensions of China's 'One Belt One Road' in Uzbekistan

by Ramtanu Maitra

Dec. 27—To seek a single purpose behind China's launch of its One Belt One Road (OBOR) project, would be as futile an exercise as that of the proverbial "six blind men of Hindustan," who attempted to describe the shape of an elephant. Some claim that Beijing's objective is to supply the want of transportation infrastructure that has prevented free movement of people and freight across the vast Eurasian landmass, divided long ago into Asia and Europe. That is true, but only partially so because, as others point out, the OBOR, in its fully developed form, will also provide energy, manufacturing, and cultural exchange, all key ingredients for society's progress and security. According to the trade journal *Supply Chain 24/7*,

> While China has invested heavily in infrastructure in recent years, investment in manufacturing has now accelerated. Beijing's aim is to upgrade its domestic industry by internationalizing it. Manufacturing outsourcing more than doubled in 2015 with machinery manufacturing increasing 154 per cent.[1]

Considering the impact of OBOR on Uzbekistan, it seems the second group of "blind men" has the advantage over the first in their quest for the complex answer. In other words, China's role in Uzbekistan does not center around running a railroad from China to Uzbekistan, but in strengthening Uzbekistan's still fragile industrial base. Of equal importance are the efforts by both nations to reestablish the old and virtually forgotten cultural linkages and develop a new linkage in science and technology.

The Historical Trade Routes

More than 2,000 years ago, at least two of the numerous trade routes across Asia passed through what is today Uzbekistan. Caravans of hundreds of Bactrian camels, often led by Sogdian merchants, would wend their way to and from China, India, and what today we call the Middle East. From China, bolts of silk went westward from about 100 B.C. to 1500 A.D. The routes and modes of conveyance were many. This web of routes that we call the Silk Road could just as easily have been described as—

> a 'Lapis Lazuli Road' from Afghanistan to Egypt and India, a 'Jade Road' from Khotan to China, an 'Emerald Road' stretching east and west from the Pamir mountains of Tajikistan and Afghanistan, or a 'Gold Road' or 'Copper Road' to the capitals of the Middle East.[2]

In the past, great Uzbek cities such as Tashkent (known as Chash, then), Ferghana (Farghona), Samarkand (Samarqand), Bukhara (Bukhoro), Khiva, and Termez emerged along these trade routes. These were then the international transshipment points, the vital centers of trade, skilled craft work, and cultural exchange, even while political rule of the region shifted from the Iranian Sogdians to the Islamic Caliphate, and then to various embodiments of Mongol and Turkic rule. Uzbekistan was absorbed into the Russian Empire in the 19th Century and became part of the Soviet Union.[3] This history is reflected in the Uzbek language, a Turkic language with influences from Persian, Arabic, Tatar, and Russian.

1. Qu Hongbin, "China Ramps Up Its Silk Road Initiative," *Supply Chain 24/7*, Dec. 22, 2016. http://www.supplychain247.com/article/china_ramps_up_its_silk_road_initiative

2. S. Frederick Starr, *Lost Enlightenment: Central Asia's Golden Age from the Arab Conquest to Tamerlane* (Princeton University Press: 2013), p. 43.
3. Rafis Abazov, *The Palgrave Concise Historical Atlas of Central Asia* (New York: Palgrave Macmillan: 2008).

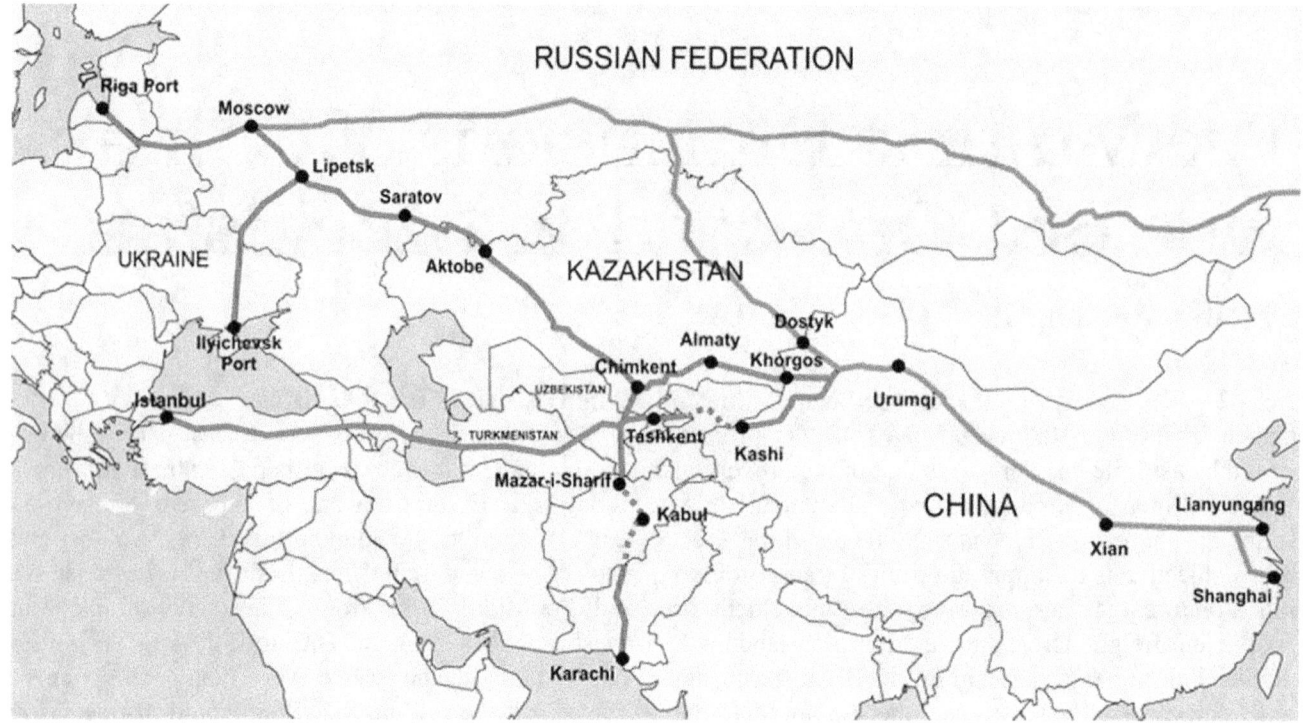

The rail links from China to and through Central Asia. The proposed segment across Kyrgyzstan, from Kashi to the Uzbekistan border near Tashkent (a dashed line), is in political limbo.

Uzbekistan, China, and Russia Today

Today, Uzbekistan is a nation of 30 million. The vast majority live in the eastern and southern part of the country; the vast arid zone of central and western Uzbekistan virtually uninhabited.

As during the golden age of Central Asia—7th to 14th centuries—Uzbekistan's bilateral trade with China to the east remains crucially important. In the first decade following Uzbekistan's independence in 1991, the value of its annual trade with China did not exceed $140 million. It gained momentum in the early 2000s and amounted to $4 billion in 2015 (20% of its total international trade).

China's One Belt, One Road initiative is now interlinked with Uzbekistan's model for economic development. China has promised investments in railroads, roads, tunnels, and other transportation projects. Some of these projects are already complete.

Throughout the Central Asian region—that is, east of the Caspian Sea—the OBOR, in conjunction with Russia to the north, is playing an important role, fortified in the recent years by the formation and strengthening of the Shanghai Cooperation Organization (SCO), an organization that includes four of the five Central Asian countries and is led by Russia and China. (The fifth, Turkmenistan, currently attends SCO meetings as a guest.)

Since the early 1990s, following the demise of the Soviet Union and emergence of these Central Asian nations as independent countries, a well-organized effort was launched from abroad, particularly from Saudi Arabia and some Gulf Sunni countries, to spread Wahhabism, a heretical deviation from Islam, in its most virulent form, throughout Central Asia. Fighters were trained, arms were provided, and an organization of some sort was set up to undermine the newly independent and politically weak nations. That not only posed an existential threat to the Central Asian countries, but rang alarm bells in Moscow and Beijing. Since the appearance of the Saudi-funded *jihadi*s, supported by London and Washington, violence has been used to weaken the political developmental process, bring economic growth to a halt, and even threaten the very ingredients necessary for future economic growth.

In this context, China's OBOR provides hope of strong future development because its mutually beneficial features have begun to emerge. China's investments in infrastructure and in developing cadre of skilled manpower in these countries go hand-in-glove with the Russian efforts to provide on-the-ground security using its vast security apparatus and with the work

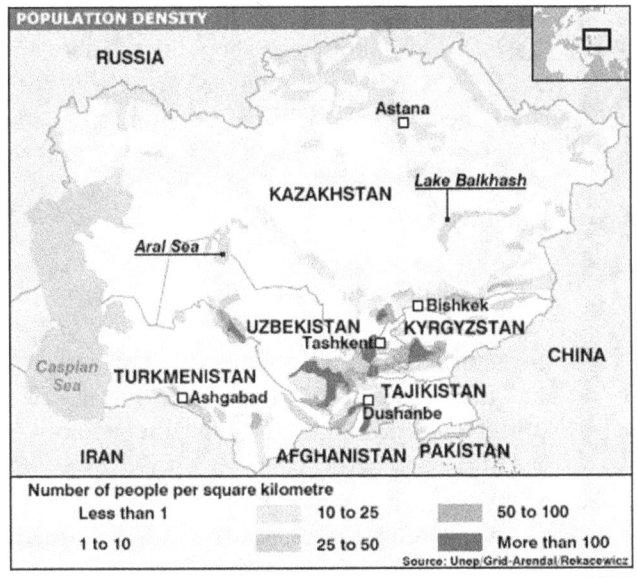

Population density map for Central Asia.

of the SCO. The success of Russia's efforts is of equal importance to that of the OBOR. Russia, situated north of these Central Asian countries and bordering Kazakhstan, is fully cognizant of these countries' topography and demography, and is an important trade partner.

China's Natural Gas and Other Investments

China's OBOR-related investments in Uzbekistan span a range of sectors. One prominent field of investment is in developing Uzbekistan's natural gas reserves and gas transportation infrastructure. This features the Central Asia-China gas pipeline, of which Uzbekistan is the linchpin: All three lines run through Uzbek territory, as will the fourth (Line D), currently under construction. The three existing lines, A, B, and C, already supply 55 billion cubic meters of natural gas a year to China. This constitutes 20 percent of China's annual natural gas consumption. These lines, already the largest liquefied natural gas (LNG) network in Central Asia, will supply another 30 billion cubic meters annually when Line D is completed, further increasing China's dependence on trans-Uzbek pipelines.

In addition, Chinese investments in the economy of Uzbekistan exceed $6.5 billion. More than 600 enterprises in Uzbekistan operate with Chinese capital. Significant joint projects have been implemented, including in the Jizzakh and Angren economic and industrial zones.[4]

---

4. Mirzokhid Rakhimov, "Dynamics of Uzbek-Chinese Relations,"

Uzbekistan on the New Silk Road

China's OBOR has identified the importance of building a railroad linking Kashgar (Kashi), in its Xinjiang province, to Uzbekistan by way of Kyrgyzstan, which lies between them. It would form a southern spur from the rail line that travels across Xinjiang to Kazakhstan, and would run from Kashgar in Xinjiang through the Arpa valley via Kyrgyzstan's Kara-Suu town, and on to the Uzbekistan city of Andijan in the Ferghana Valley. At present, there is no direct rail link between China and Uzbekistan through Kyrgyzstan, which "considerably complicates the freight transport between the two countries," according to Sofia Pale of the Russian Academy of Sciences.[5]

Pale explains the importance of the direct link:

In addition to the export of Chinese goods to local markets, China has plans to use the Kyrgyz rail links to import hydrocarbons from Uzbekistan and earth metals, iron, copper, and aluminum ores, coal and uranium from Kyrgyzstan. Given China's desire to reach the largest possible area in order to increase its turnover, it is not surprising that the idea of building a railway linking China, Kyrgyzstan, and Uzbekistan will soon be put into action by the Chinese. The project is to connect China not only with Uzbekistan via Kyrgyzstan, but also with Tajikistan, and then rail track will be laid through Afghanistan, Iran, and Turkey, until finally, they can be connected to the European railway network. Incidentally, China has chosen the European standard gauge for this task, not Russian.

The "earth metals" referred to here are usually called the "rare earth metals," which include scandium, yttrium, and the 15 lanthanide elements on the Mendeleev Periodic Table.

China.org.cn, June 21, 2016. http://www.china.org.cn/opinion/2016-06/21/content_38708678.htm

5. Sofia Pale, "Kyrgyzstan and the Chinese 'New Silk Road'," *New Eastern Outlook*, Sept. 3, 2015. http://journal-neo.org/2015/09/03/kyrgyzstan-and-the-chinese-new-silk-road/ However, the Kyrgyz trading town of Kara-Suu, located close to the Uzbek border, serves as a vital link to Uzbekistan: It is situated on the interregional highway that links the Kyrgyz capital of Bishkek, Osh, and the capital of China's Xinjiang province, Urumqi. There is also a railroad that links the administrative and economic center Jalal-Abad in southwestern Kyrgyzstan to the Uzbek town of Andijan and runs through Kara-Suu, but it is not connected to the rail line to Urumqi.

The Qamchiq Tunnel in the Angren-Pap railroad in Uzbekistan.

Political Roadblocks

Kyrgyz President Almazbek Atambayev showed a great deal of enthusiasm for the railroad in 2012, and in early 2015, after prolonged talks, a route linking China, Kyrgyzstan, and Uzbekistan was agreed. China is to build the 500 kilometer segment in Kyrgyzstan, investing $6 billion. Kyrgyzstan hopes to gain about $200 million per year from the transit of goods through its territory. On the Uzbekistan side, Uzbekistan said in September 2016 that it had finished 104 kilometers of the 129 kilometer Uzbek stretch of the railway.

Kyrgyzstan, however, is not of one mind about the project. The President himself has vacillated. Pale reports,

Many Kyrgyz officials have questioned the feasibility of the construction itself, because all work will be carried out exclusively by Chinese companies, and the railway will only start to make money for Kyrgyzstan after China's expenses have been paid off. Moreover, according to the expert on infrastructure projects in Central Eurasia, Kubat Rakhimov, the profitability of the project for Kyrgyzstan is in doubt. He believes that China is unlikely to allow someone to make money on transit. In addition, the mountainous landscape of Kyrgyzstan significantly scales up the risk of increases in construction costs.

These considerations of feasibility and profitability are "practical" arguments that seem to disregard the promise, for all partners, of the greater OBOR conception. But the real source of resistance may lie in the realm of politics and geopolitics. There are concerns that the railroad may result in "the strengthening of Uzbekistan's dominance in the region and even the probability of violation of Kyrgyzstan's territorial integrity," according to Pale. And within Kyrgyzstan,

There are unspoken contradictions between representatives of the ruling elites of the northern and southern regions of the country, and the construction of the railway could shift the balance of power in the direction of one of the competing camps.

Pale is referring to the two elites, a northern (ethnic Kyrgyz) and a southern (ethnic Uzbek). The project will run through the south of Kyrgyzstan, causing the northern elite to fear that a shift in the internal power balance may result. She also refers to the fear that a strengthened southern region could attempt to secede and that it could be encouraged to do so by Uzbekistan.

Many Kyrgyz propose that a north-south railway—Russia-Kazakhstan-Kyrgyzstan-Tajikistan—uniting the two parts of the country, must be built first; they argue that if the China-Kyrgyzstan-Uzbekistan railroad is built first, the north-south line may never be built.

These political considerations are also intertwined with geopolitical tensions—tensions between Russia and China with respect to Central Asia, and tensions aggravated by Anglo-American manipulations in the Tulip Revolution of 2005.

Kyrgyzstan will have to resolve these internal conflicts, and it is likely that China—if not also Uzbekistan, in particular—needs to take a hand in overcoming Kyrgyzstan's fears. Kyrgyzstan's situation is compounded by its weak financial condition, including heavy indebtedness. It has virtually no capital to invest.

Rail Line: Tashkent to Fergana Valley

Meanwhile, China and Uzbekistan have together developed a very important rail link between Tashkent and the Ferghana Valley. This is the Angren-Pap railway, inaugurated on June 22, 2016 by President Xi Jinping and the late Uzbek President Islam Karimov.

The highlight of this rail link is the 19.2 kilometer Qamchiq Tunnel, the longest in the 1,520 mm rail-gauge region and the key element of the project. The inaugural train from Angren to Pap (Pop)—a Chinese-built O'zbekiston electric locomotive and four coaches—passed through the tunnel in 16 minutes, according to news reports. The tunnel eliminates the need for Uzbek trains to transit Tajikistan to reach the Ferghana Valley, and provides an all-weather alternative to the road over a pass at an altitude of 2,267 meters. The rail line, built by China Railway Tunnel Group, also includes 25 bridges and 6 viaducts with a total length of 2.1 km, and four stations at Orzu, Kul, Temiryulobod, and Kushminor.

One of the 6 viaducts and 25 bridges on Uzbekistan's new Angren-Pap railway line.

Industrial Investments

The Angren-Pap railroad is destined to play an important role in Uzbekistan's industrial progress in the coming years. It will become a very important cog in the Angren Special Industrial Zone (SIZ) that includes 16 investment projects worth more than $224.8 million to be implemented in the coming years.

Located at the intersection of Uzbekistan's various transport routes close to Tashkent region, Angren SIZ has received $60 million from the Uzbek government. Over the past years, leading companies in Austria, Bulgaria, Great Britain, India, Singapore, and South Korea have partnered in commissioning enterprises specializing in the production of copper pipes of different diameters, industrial silicon, energy-saving LED lamps, coal briquettes, construction and finishing materials, and sugar. The joint enterprises have provided more than a thousand new jobs. The Uzbek-Chinese enterprise Jun Long Industrial in Angren SIZ has established the manufacture of coal briquettes from coal powder. A joint Uzbek-South Korean venture, Uz-Shindong Silicon, has been recently commissioned to produce industrial silicon. The projected cost of the plant is $8.67 million, providing about 200 new jobs. The Uzbek-South Korean company Egl-Nur is another successful example. Driven by modern technologies, the enterprise manufactures world-standard, energy-saving LED lamps.

In addition to Angren SIZ, Uzbekistan has two other long-established Free Industrial and Economic Zones, Navoi and Jizzhakh. The zone in the Navoi region (west of Tashkent and close to Bukhara) was established in 2008, and the Jizzakh zone (in the central part of the country, close to Samarkand) with its branch in Syrdarya district, was founded in 2013.

Several Chinese companies—Nan Yang Mulanhu, Henan Sine, Pinmian Co. Ltd, and Hebey An Feng Da Group—have shown interest in implementing textile-producing enterprises in the Jizzakh industrial and economic zone. Uzbekistan is the 6th largest producer of cotton in the world and cotton is its main cash crop.

According to a company representative, the total planned design capacity of the enterprises will amount to annual production of 30 million square meters of cotton fabric, 13,000 tons of knitted fabric, and 15 million garments including knitwear. Up to 80 percent of the products will be exported in accordance with the terms for creating the enterprises.

OBOR Draws in Japan and Russia

These linkages with China, developed from the Chinese initiative in the form of the OBOR, have attracted other international companies. For instance, the Japanese behemoths, Mitsubishi Corporation and Mitsubishi Hitachi Power Systems, Ltd, in October won a turnkey contract to construct the Turakurgan thermal power plant in the Namangan region of the Ferghana Valley in 2017. It will have two units, each generating 450 MW, with steam and gas turbines.

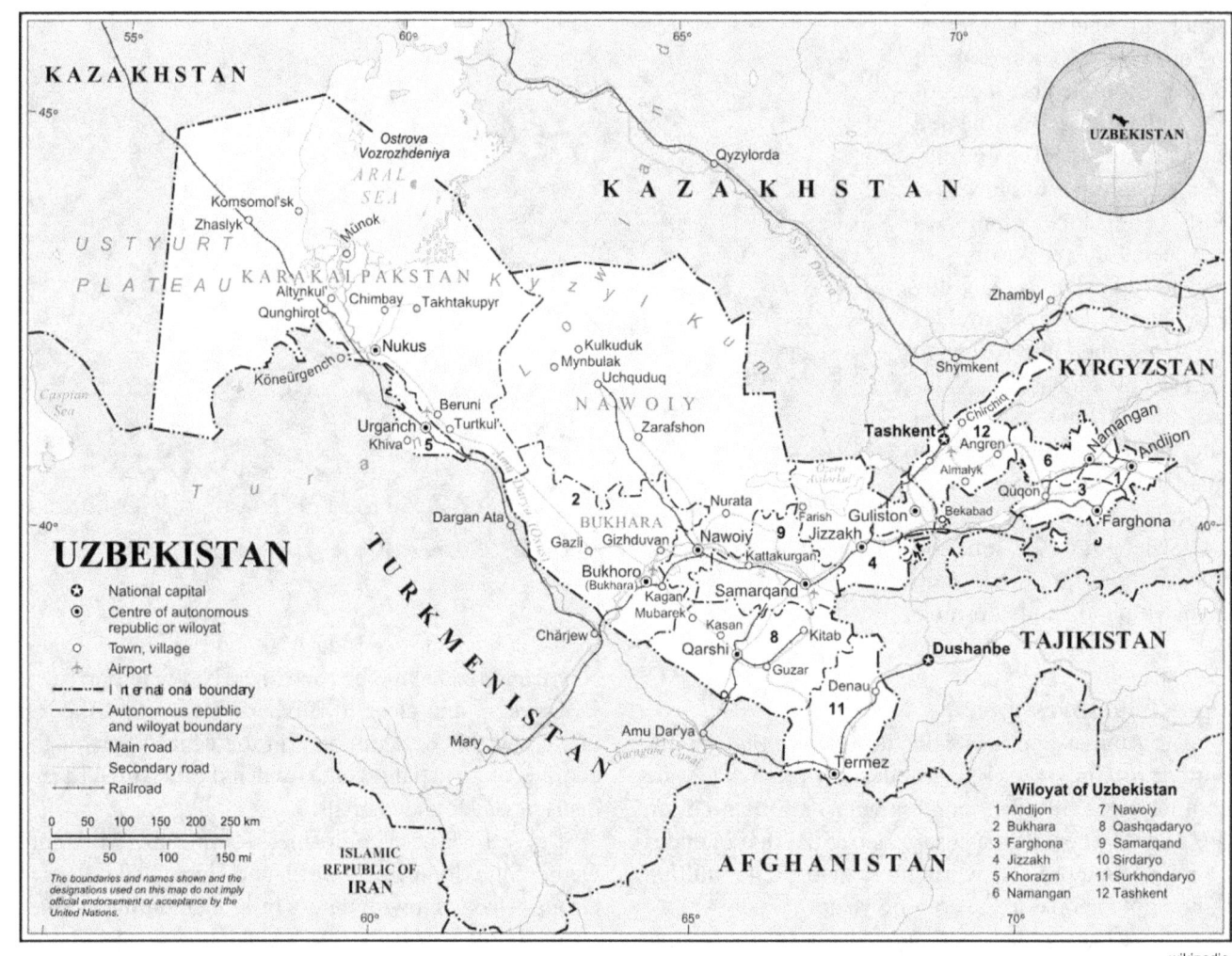

Similarly, Russia's oil company, Lukoil, announced in November an investment of $500 million for the development of the Gissar gas and gas condensate fields in the Kashkadarya Region of Uzbekistan (situated in the basin of the Kashkadarya (river) on the western slopes of the Pamir Alay Mountains, bordered by Turkmenistan and Tajikistan).

The Cultural Dimension

One of the most important contributions of the OBOR is the exchange of cultural traditions among the countries that are becoming interlinked through railroads. In some cases, as in the case of Uzbekistan and China, the task involves reviving the long-lost cultural exchanges that took place when the Silk Road and other trade routes were alive in the past.

In the 20th century, Tashkent, the capital of Uzbekistan, served throughout the Soviet period as a center for Chinese studies. Beginning in 1957, people from all over Central Asia came to Tashkent to learn Mandarin. Since becoming independent in 1991, Uzbekistan has received support from the Chinese government to continue teaching Mandarin. The Confucius Institute in Tashkent, which opened in 2005, is not only the first Confucius Institute in Uzbekistan, but also the first in Central Asia. Like other Confucius Institutes around the world, its mission is to promote the teaching of Mandarin and develop cultural and educational exchanges between China and the host country. Now the study of Chinese is viewed in Uzbekistan as advantageous for business and for professional employment abroad, and many students hope to get stipends to study in China.[6]

---

6. Julie Yu-Wen Chen and Olaf Günther, "China's Influence in Uzbekistan: Model Neighbor or Indifferent Partner?" Jamestown Foundation, *China Brief* 16:17 (November 11, 2016). https://jamestown.org/program/chinas-influence-uzbekistan-model-neighbor-indifferent-partner/

Putin in Japan—A Transformation of Asia

by Michael Billington

Dec. 24—President Vladimir Putin's visit to Japan on Dec. 15-16, meeting with Japanese Prime Minister Shinzo Abe first in Abe's home prefecture of Yamaguchi, then in Tokyo, has solidified a positive transformation of relations between the two nations taking place over the past year. This process has linked Japan firmly into the development of the Russian Far East, while also demonstrating that Japan is capable of acting independently from the British imperial policies which have dominated Washington over the last 16 years of misrule under George Bush and Barack Obama.

This transformation extends beyond the bilateral ties between

kremlin.ru

Russian President Vladimir Putin (left) welcomes Japan Prime Minister Shinzo Abe to Russia on Dec. 15, 2016, for serious strategic talks.

the two nations, contributing to a general shift of the entirety of Asia away from the divisions created by the Obama policy of encircling China and Russia economically and militarily, which has brought the world to the brink of thermonuclear war. Instead, Asia is increasingly united behind the new paradigm of peaceful development and cooperation, centered on the New Silk Road process set in motion by China and fully supported by Russia.

While the festering territorial issues—which have prevented the signing of a peace treaty between Japan and Russia since World War II—were not settled during the Putin visit, the path to a solution was firmly established. It is based on joint development of the contested Kuril Islands (called the Northern Territories in Japan), and huge Japanese investment and infrastructure development within Russia.

Two Japans

Lyndon LaRouche has always insisted that there are two Japans. First, the Japan of the Meiji Restoration, heavily influenced by the American Hamiltonian system, which was introduced to Japan by economist E. Peshine Smith. He served as the first foreign advisor to the Meiji government from 1871-1876. Smith—a friend of American System economist (and Lincoln advi-

E. Peshine Smith, American System economist, was employed by the Meiji Government 1871-1876.

sor) Henry Carey—aided in the transformation of Japan from a feudal society to a modern industrial power.

The second Japan emerged under the influence of the British Empire, which convinced some Japanese leaders of the Meiji that, as an island nation like the British, it must become an Empire, militarily colonizing other nations, in order to have access to the raw materials it would need. This faction led to the horrors of World War II, begining with Japan's military occupation of much of China in the 1930s.

Post-war Japan, under the tutelage of Gen. Douglas MacArthur, returned to being the Japan of peaceful development, rapidly becoming one of the world's greatest industrial powers, while retaining a constitutional restriction against waging war. The current Prime Minister Shinzo Abe's grandfather, Nobusuke Kishi, who served as a post-war Prime Minister from 1957-60, and Shinzo Abe's father, Shintaro Abe, Foreign Minister from 1982-86, both made efforts to restore relations with Russia, despite the British-American Cold War hysteria against Russia at that time.

Nobusuke Kishi (left), the maternal grandfather of Shinzo Abe, was the 56th and 57th Prime Minister of Japan. Shintaro Abe, Shinzo Abe's father (right) was Japan's longest reigning postwar foreign minister. Both father and grandfather were committed to developing good relations with Russia.

The primary conflict between Japan and Russia was (and still is) the issue of sovereignty over the Kuril Islands (Northern Territories), the four islands north of Hokkaido in the Kamchatka island chain, which were occupied and claimed by the Soviet Union near the end of World War II. In 1956, Japan and the USSR reached an agreement to divide the islands—two to each side— but U.S. Secretary of State John Foster Dulles, who served as a spokesman for British imperial interests throughout his life, threatened Japan that if it failed to demand sovereignty over all four islands, the United States would renege on its pledge to return Okinawa to Japanese sovereignty.

After that, the USSR, and post-USSR Russia, refused to renew their offer to divide the islands. A second effort at reaching a similar agreement in 2000 also ended with Japan walking away from the discussions— probably under U.S. pressure.

President Putin clearly understands this problem—

that Japan is still an occupied country in some respects, one which has sometimes acted against its own interests due to pressure from Washington. In an interview with *Yomiuri Shimbun* and Nippon TV in Moscow on Dec. 13, just before his trip, Putin responded to questions about his expectations for reaching an agreement by touching on this reality in his reply:

Look, I have just said we have the highest bilateral turnover and continue liberalizing our trade ties, as you know. However, Japan imposed economic sanctions against us. Do you see the difference? Why? Due to the events in Ukraine or in Syria? However, Japan and Russian-Japanese relations are hardly related to the events in Syria or in Ukraine. Therefore, Japan has some alliance obligations. We treat them with respect, but we need to understand the degree of Japan's freedom and what steps it is ready to take. We should look into this, as these are not minor issues. Our foundation for signing a peace agreement will depend on them. This is the difference between current Russian-Japanese and, for instance, Russian-Chinese relations. I do not want to argue; you asked me what the point is. The point is to create an atmosphere of trust.

The New Paradigm

Nonetheless, Putin has welcomed Abe's call for renewing the 1956 framework, indicating that after a period of joint development of the islands, and visits there by former Japanese residents, businessmen, and tourists, the concept of returning two of the islands can again serve as a basis for a final determination and a peace treaty.

The process between these two leaders during 2016 was fascinating. It began with a visit by Abe to meet Putin in Sochi in May. Despite Obama's insistence that Abe not hold such a meeting, the two leaders met, and expressed a commitment to resolve all outstanding

kremlin.ru

Putin and Abe emerging from a working session on Dec. 15, 2016.

issues and proceed with cooperative development. Japan had imposed minor, token sanctions on Russia under pressure from Obama after the U.S.-orchestrated coup in Ukraine, but Putin essentially ignored that as rather unimportant.

Sources in Japan who are close to both the Japanese and Russian governments told *EIR* at the time, that the sovereignty issue would only be discussed privately, but that the path to a resolution in 2017 or 2018 would be set in motion as joint development proceeded.

Lyndon LaRouche, in reviewing the eight-point joint Japan-Russia development proposal put forth by Abe in Sochi, asked: "Is Japan really going to do this? If so, that's a very positive development for the entirety of Asia."

The proposal for Russia's Far East included oil and gas development, medical facilities, transportation, port development, and more.

Western Economic Crisis

Soon after the Sochi visit, Japan hosted the annual G-7 Summit—without Russia, since Russia had been thrown out of the former G-8. At that Summit, Abe challenged Obama and the other G-7 leaders by refusing to go along with their fraudulent hype that the western economies were doing fine, that a steady recovery was on the way, and that the insane speculative binge driving the trans-Atlantic financial system to the brink did not exist.

Abe spoiled the party, telling the Summit that there

was a severe risk "of falling into a crisis if we did not take appropriate policy responses in a timely manner." He told the press after the event that "We're facing a big crisis and big risks." *Yomiuri Shimbun* reported that: "The Prime Minister compared the current situation to the one that existed before the global financial crisis triggered by the collapse of Lehman brothers." Abe called for a concerted fiscal stimulus by the other G-7 nations, pointing precisely to his proposals for the development of the vast Russian Far East, and Japan's other investments in Asia, as a model.

Obama and the British would hear none of it. Bloomberg gloated that "Japanese Prime Minister Abe failed in his bid to have the G-7 leaders warn of the risk of a global economic crisis in a communiqué issued as their Summit wraps up." Instead, the communiqué expressed the fantasy that the G-7 countries "have strengthened the resilience of our economies in order to avoid falling into another crisis."

Abe then travelled to Vladivostok in September to attend the Eastern Economic Forum, at which he focused on the development of the Russian Far East, during another private meeting with Putin. Eighteen development projects in five categories were discussed and presented to the press, which included airports, Advanced Special Economic Zones, Free Port cooperation, joint funds for urban development, joint industrial parks, a Sakhalin-Hokkaido power and transport bridge or tunnel, and cooperation on the development of an Arctic sea route.

Essentially all of these projects were approved during Putin's December visit to Japan—and more. More than 60 projects and cooperation agreements were signed, totalling about $2.5 billion, and a joint investment fund of $1 billion was established, with plans to launch 20 projects in the first half of 2017.

Beside plans for building a Sakhalin-Hokkaido rail connection, Japan may help build a tunnel connecting Sakhalin to the Russian mainland. Together these two tunnels would link all of Japan to the Trans-Siberian Railroad, and thus to all of Eurasia by rail, thus linking to the new rail routes being built under the Chinese Belt and Road Initiative.

Nuclear cooperation is also on the table, as Russia's Rosatom State Atomic Energy Corporation signed an agreement for peaceful nuclear power development with Japan's Ministry of Economy, Trade, and Industry, including an expansion of Russia's supply of enriched uranium to Japan.

The joint statement signed by Putin and Abe included the statement: "The start of consultation on joint economic activity of Russia and Japan on the South Kuril Islands may become an important step towards signing a peace treaty."

kremlin.ru

Putin and Abe at the conclusion of their talks.

The Governors of Russia's Sakhalin Region and Japan's Hokkaido Prefecture met on Dec. 18, and Sakhalin Governor Oleg Kozhemyako said: "We are ready to provide Japanese companies with an opportunity to implement various projects in the South Kuril Islands that would cover housing construction, road-building, setting up waste recycling facilities, and developing aquaculture."

In an interview with TASS following Putin's visit, Abe said: "From my Grandfather [Prime Minister Kishi] I learnt that if this is a policy that you believe is right—if this is a conclusion to which you came as a result of thorough considerations—then you need to conduct it decisively and firmly, and sometimes with a danger for life."

Regarding the agreements with Putin, he added: "I think that it is the Japanese-Russian relations that have the most of all possibilities, and it can be said that these possibilities are unlimited."

China's Role

The historic significance of this new relationship for all of Asia, and the world, has been largely ignored in the West, and when it is reported on, it is described as an effort by Japan to work with Russia as a "hedge against the rise of China," with the claim that both Russia and Japan are worried about the supposed China threat.

In fact, in his interview with *Yomiuri Shimbun* in

Moscow before his trip to Japan, Putin strongly asserted the extremely strong strategic partnership between Russia and China, indicating that such a level of trust was the necessary basis for moving relations between Russia and Japan forward. He noted his deep respect for Japanese culture (emphasizing his love of judo since his childhood), but insisted that he loves Russia more, and must act on the basis of Russia's fundamental interests.

While the distrust between China and Japan since World War II is far more difficult to overcome than that between Japan and Russia, it is precisely the cooperation among nations on large-scale physical development projects which has formed the basis for China's Belt and Road Initiative, including an invitation to Japan (and the United States) to participate. China is legitimately concerned about Abe's effort to drop Japan's Constitutional restriction against war, allowing Japan to join in foreign wars, such as any potential U.S. war on China. However, Abe has, over the last year, pulled back on his push for such a change—under strong domestic and international opposition—although, for him, it remains a serious concern.

Using the Silk Road concept as the basis for win-win cooperation among nations, we can, and must, replace the imperial concepts of geopolitics, zero-sum competition, and conflict among the world's nations and peoples. The Russia-Japan agreements provide another dramatic step towards that vision for the future.